Foreword

In a world where technological advancement is rapidly escalating, the race to understand the complexities of the human brain takes center stage. "Neuro-Symbolism: Mathematical Formulas for Decoding Brain Functions and Advancing AI" serves as a crucial cornerstone for scholars and practitioners who are at the intersection of neuroscience, cognitive psychology, and artificial intelligence. This book delves into a comprehensive framework that symbolically represents complex neurobiological processes and cognitive functions, providing a structured approach to understand the brain's architecture. By equipping scholars with these mathematical tools, the book not only helps to decode the underlying processes of cognitive phenomena but also contributes significantly to the development of emergent AI technologies.

Larry Matthews

Preface

We live in an era where the fusion of neuroscience and artificial intelligence is not just a possible future—it's a present reality. Yet the gap between our understanding of the human brain and our ability to mimic its functions in AI systems remains wide. This book aims to bridge that gap by introducing scholars to a variety of advanced mathematical models that shed light on neurocognitive processes. From fundamental concepts of neuronal spiking to the intricacies of emotional systems, the book covers a spectrum of topics that will allow you to grasp the essence of the human mind computationally. As you navigate through these pages, you will encounter equations and formulas specifically designed to help you understand and document the myriad functions of the brain, thereby improving your capacity to contribute to the field of artificial intelligence.

Table of Contents

Chapter 1 - Symbolic Representation of Neurobiological Processes in Cognitive Functions

Symbolic Representation of Neurobiological Processes in Cognitive Functions
Mathematical and computational models have increasingly aided the field of neuroscience to describe the complex processes occurring in the brain. These models range from simplified abstractions to detailed biophysical descriptions of neural activity. Utilizing symbolic representation to describe various brain actions provides a powerful framework for understanding and predicting brain functions (Dayan Abbott, 2001; Gerstner, Kistler, Naud, Paninski, 2014).

Voltage Spike Generation by Neurons
The production of voltage spikes by neurons can be mathematically captured using the piecewise function:

$$V_n(t) = \{V_{spike} \; if \, a \, spike \, occurs \, at \, time \, t \; 0 \, otherwise$$

where $V_n(t)$ denotes the voltage produced by neuron n at time t, and V_{spike} is the voltage level during a spike. This representation is a simplification of the more complex Hodgkin-Huxley model, but provides a foundational understanding of spike generation (Hodgkin Huxley, 1952).

Axonal Pulse Propagation
The propagation of a neural pulse along an axon can be expressed as:

$$P(t) = V_n(t - \tau)$$

where $P(t)$ denotes the pulse at time t, and τ represents the time delay associated with pulse propagation. This model could be extended to include the effects of myelination and axonal diameter on signal speed (Seidl, 2014).

Synaptic Chemical Signal Release
The release of neurotransmitters at the synapse can be described as:

$$S(t) = \alpha \cdot V_n(t)$$

where $S(t)$ is the chemical signal strength at time t, and α is a coefficient translating the voltage to chemical signal strength. This offers a linear approximation to the complex mechanisms of synaptic neurotransmission (Koch, 1999).

Facial Recognition
The cognitive task of recognizing a face can be symbolically represented as:

$$R(x) = \{1 \; if \, face \, is \, recognized \; 0 \, otherwise$$

where $R(x)$ is a function of the input x, which could be a multidimensional vector representing the visual data of a face. Recent advances in neural decoding techniques have focused on reconstructing perceived images from brain activity, offering a bridge between this symbolic representation and empirical data (Naselaris et al., 2015).

Memory States
Different types of memory, including short-term, long-term, and declarative memories, can be conceptually represented as a state vector in a memory space:

$$M = MshortMlongMdeclarative$$

Each component of this vector may be subject to different rules for updating and decay, governed by various biochemical and electrical processes (Fuster, 1995; Squire, 2009).

In summary, symbolic representations offer a useful lens for conceptualizing complex neurobiological processes. These representations may serve as the foundation for more detailed models, incorporating empirical findings from both experimental and computational neuroscience.

References

- Dayan, P., Abbott, L. F. (2001). Theoretical neuroscience: computational and mathematical modeling of neural systems. MIT press. - Gerstner, W., Kistler, W. M., Naud, R., Paninski, L. (2014). Neuronal dynamics: From single neurons to networks and models of cognition. Cambridge University Press. Hodgkin, A. L., Huxley, A. F. (1952). A quantitative description of membrane current and its application to conduction and excitation in nerve. The Journal of physiology, 117(4), 500-544. - Koch, C. (1999). Biophysics of computation: Information processing in single neurons. Oxford University Press, USA. - Seidl, A. H. (2014). Regulation of conduction time along axons. Neuroscience, 276, 126-134. - Naselaris, T., Kay, K. N., Nishimoto, S., Gallant, J. L. (2015). Encoding and decoding in fMRI. NeuroImage, 56(2), 400-410. - Fuster, J. M. (1995). Memory in the cerebral cortex: an empirical approach to neural networks in the human and nonhuman primate. MIT Press. - Squire, L. R. (2009). Memory and brain systems: 1969–2009. The Journal of neuroscience, 29(41), 12711-12716.

Chapter 2 - Extended Symbolic Representations for Cognitive and Neurological Phenomena

The complexity of the brain's operations can be further understood through additional symbolic representations that account for various forms of learning, memory dynamics, sensory associations, and baseline activities. These models can build upon foundational concepts in computational neuroscience and cognitive psychology (O'Reilly Munakata, 2000; Friston, 2010).

Learning and Memory as Functions of Brain Structures

Different memory types can be described as functions dependent on various brain structures:

$$M_i = f_i(B)$$

Here, M_i signifies the i-th type of memory, and B represents a vector comprising the relevant brain structures. This perspective aligns with the growing research on the localization and distribution of different memory systems within the brain (Eichenbaum, 2017).

Synaptic Changes for Memory Storage

The strengthening or weakening of synaptic connections, fundamental to memory storage, can be modeled as:

$$S_{ij}(t) = w \cdot A_i(t) \cdot A_j(t)$$

In this equation, $S_{ij}(t)$ denotes the strength of the synaptic connection between neurons i and j at time t, while $A_i(t)$ and $A_j(t)$ represent their respective neural activities. The term w serves as a weight parameter. This formula encapsulates the essence of Hebbian learning rules, which are pivotal in synaptic plasticity (Hebb, 1949).

Associations and Sensory Triggers

Associative learning can be represented by a vector $\mathbf{C}$ that encapsulates various sensations:

$$\mathbf{C} = CsmellCtasteCcolorCfeel$$

An associated triggering equation is:

$$C_{trigger} = \mathbf{M} \cdot \mathbf{C}$$

Here, $\mathbf{M}$ is a matrix that signifies how one sensation can evoke another. This formulation offers a mathematical perspective on classical conditioning paradigms (Pavlov, 1927).

Encoding Relationships

Encoding can be abstractly represented by a function that captures relationships between elements:

$$E(\mathbf{r}) = \mathbf{R}$$

In this expression, **r** is a vector containing raw data, while **R** is a vector of relationships between these elements. This concept aligns with theories of relational memory (Cohen Eichenbaum, 1993).

Memory Retrieval

The process of memory retrieval can be modeled as:

$$\mathbf{m} = R(\mathbf{q})$$

Here, **m** is the retrieved memory and **q** is the query. This symbolic representation could include probabilistic or dynamic retrieval aspects (Anderson, 1983).
Memory Destabilization

The transient destabilization of memory can be expressed as:

$$\mathbf{M}_{temp} = D(\mathbf{m})$$

Here, $\mathbf{M}_{temp}$ represents the temporarily destabilized memory, and D is a function denoting the destabilization process. This equation resonates with research on memory reconsolidation (Nader, Schafe, Le Doux, 2000).

Baseline Brain Activity

Baseline neural activity can be described by the function:

$$B(t) = k \cdot R(t) + b$$

In this equation, $B(t)$ denotes the baseline brain activity at time t, $R(t)$ indicates restructuring or simulating knowledge, k is a scaling constant, and b represents other baseline activities. This formulation can incorporate fluctuating baseline activities observed in resting-state networks (Raichle, 2015).

References

- O'Reilly, R. C., Munakata, Y. (2000). Computational explorations in cognitive neuroscience: Understanding the mind by simulating the brain. MIT press. - Friston, K. (2010). The free-energy principle: a unified brain theory? Nature reviews neuroscience, 11(2), 127-138. - Eichenbaum, H. (2017). Memory: Organization and control. Annual Review of Psychology, 68, 19-45. Hebb, D. O. (1949). The organization of behavior. Wiley. - Pavlov, I. P. (1927). Conditioned reflexes. Oxford University Press. - Cohen, N. J., Eichenbaum, H. (1993). Memory, amnesia, and the hippocampal system. MIT press. - Anderson, J. R. (1983). Retrieval of information from long-term memory. Science, 220(4592), 25-30. - Nader, K., Schafe, G. E., Le Doux, J. E. (2000). Fear memories require protein synthesis in the amygdala for reconsolidation after retrieval. Nature, 406(6797), 722-726. - Raichle, M. E. (2015). The restless brain: how intrinsic activity organizes brain function. Philosophical Transactions of the Royal Society B: Biological Sciences, 370(1668), 20140172.

Chapter 3 - Further Expansions in Symbolic Representations of Neurocognitive Processes

To comprehensively model the rich tapestry of cognitive and neurobiological processes, we extend the symbolic framework to include task-oriented behavior, perception, dreaming, and predictive faculties. These mathematical models aim to capture the multi-faceted nature of mental activities and are influenced by contemporary research in neuroscience and cognitive science (Friston, 2009; Hassabis Maguire, 2009).

Preparatory Activity Reduction for Goal-Directed Tasks
The rate of change in baseline neural activity before executing a goal directed task can be represented as:

$$B'(t) = -\delta \cdot G(t)$$

Here, $B'(t)$ is the rate of change of baseline activity, $G(t)$ is a function describing the goal-directed task, and δ is a constant determining the rate of activity decrease. This model can be interpreted in light of research on preparatory activity in neural networks (Bastian et al., 2003).

Sensory Input and Internal Experience Perceived sensory experience can be described by:

$$P(t) = S(t) + I(t)$$

In this equation, $P(t)$ is the perceived experience at time t, $S(t)$ is the internal sensory state, and $I(t)$ is the external sensory input. This reflects theories suggesting that perception is a function of both external stimuli and internal states (Chalmers, 1996).
Awake and Dream States

The *awake state* can be modeled as a weighted combination of the dreaming state and external stimuli:

$$A(t) = D(t) + \square \cdot E(t)$$

Here, $A(t)$ is the awake state at time t, $D(t)$ represents the dreaming state, $E(t)$ is external stimuli, and $\square$ is a constant. This model aligns with theories of dreaming as a form of proto-consciousness (Hobson, 2009).

Emulating Possible Futures
The emulation of possible future states can be represented as:

$$F(t,a) = E(S(t),a)$$

In this representation, $F(t,a)$ is the future state at time t given an action a, $S(t)$ is the current state, and E is an emulation function. This is relevant to discussions on mental time travel and planning (Schacter, Addis, Buckner, 2007).

Internal Representations of External Reality

The brain's internal model of the external world can be encapsulated by:

$$M(t) = I(t) \cdot R$$

Here, $M(t)$ is the internal model at time t, $I(t)$ is the sensory input, and R is a matrix that formalizes the relationships between various elements in the external world. This is consistent with theories of internal models in cognition (Wolpert, Ghahramani, Jordan, 1995).

Perception as Expectation Matching

Perception can be modeled as a matching process between incoming sensory data and internal expectations:

$$P(t) = M(I(t), E(t))$$

Here, $P(t)$ is the perceived experience at time t, $I(t)$ is incoming sensory data, $E(t)$ is internally generated expectations, and M is a matching function.
This notion is foundational to predictive coding theories of brain function (Rao Ballard, 1999).

Memory for Predictive Functions

Memory can be conceptualized as a tool for generating predictions, expressed as:

$$\Pi(t) = P(M(t))$$

In this equation, $\Pi(t)$ is the prediction at time t, $M(t)$ is the memory at that time, and P is a function converting memories into predictions. This representation extends theories that posit memory as an essential element in future planning and prediction (Bar, 2009).

References
- Friston, K. (2009). The free-energy principle: a rough guide to the brain? Trends in cognitive sciences, 13(7), 293-301. - Hassabis, D., Maguire, E. A. (2009). The construction system of the brain. Philosophical Transactions of the Royal Society B: Biological Sciences, 364(1521), 1263-1271. - Bastian, A., Sch"oner, G., Riehle, A. (2003). Preshaping and continuous evolution of motor cortical representations during movement preparation. The European Journal of Neuroscience, 18(7), 2047-2058. - Chalmers, D. J. (1996). The conscious mind: In search of a fundamental theory. Oxford University Press. - Hobson, J. A. (2009). REM sleep and dreaming: towards a theory of protoconsciousness. Nature Reviews Neuroscience, 10(11), 803-813. - Schacter, D. L., Addis, D. R., Buckner, R. L. (2007). Remembering the past to imagine the future: the prospective brain. Nature Reviews Neuroscience, 8(9), 657-661. - Wolpert, D. M., Ghahramani, Z., Jordan, M. I. (1995). An internal model for sensorimotor integration. Science, 269(5232), 1880-1882. - Rao, R. P., Ballard, D. H. (1999). Predictive coding in the visual cortex: a functional interpretation of some extra-classical receptive-field effects. Nature neuroscience, 2(1), 79-87. Bar, M. (2009). The proactive brain: memory for predictions. Philosophical Transactions of the Royal Society B: Biological Sciences, 364(1521), 1235-1243.

Chapter 4 - Incorporating Emotional Dimensions in Symbolic Representations of Neurocognitive Phenomena

Integrating emotional components into mathematical models of brain functions contributes to a more comprehensive understanding of cognitive and affective processes. In this context, we introduce new symbolic representations that capture the role of emotions and feelings in cognition, rooted in contemporary neuroscience and psychology perspectives (Damasio, 1994; LeDoux, 1996).

Special Subtype of Emulation: Memory of Life Events

A specialized form of the emulation function, tailored to represent memories of life events, can be expressed as:

$$F_{life}(t,a) = E(S(t),a;constraints)$$

Here, constraints are introduced to ensure that the emulation progresses in a manner consistent with life experiences. This resonates with theories positing that episodic memories may serve as a basis for simulating future events (Schacter et al., 2008).

Emotions as Physical Responses to Stimuli

Emotions can be modeled as a response function to various stimuli, and are represented as:

$$E(t) = R(S(t))$$

In this equation, $E(t)$ is the emotion at time t, $S(t)$ represents the stimulus, and R is a function mapping stimuli to physical reactions such as heart rate or perspiration. This formulation is aligned with the James-Lange theory of emotion (James, 1884; Lange, 1885).

Feelings as Subjective Transformations of Emotions

The subjective nature of feelings can be captured by transforming physical emotions into subjective experiences:

$$F(t) = F(E(t))$$

Here, $F(t)$ signifies the feeling at time t, and F is a function translating physical emotions into subjective experiences. This concept is informed by theories distinguishing between emotions and feelings (Damasio, 1999).

Emotions as Computational Drivers of Action

The role of emotions in guiding actions can be formalized as:

$$A(t) = C(E(t),O(t))$$

In this equation, $A(t)$ is the action at time t, $O(t)$ represents the outcome, and C is a function that incorporates emotions and anticipated outcomes to determine actions. This is consistent with models positing that emotions serve as computations for action selection (Cosmides Tooby, 2000).

Emotional Influence on Perception
The influence of emotion on perception can be represented as:

$$P'(t) = P(t) + \alpha \cdot E(t)$$

Here, $P'(t)$ is the modified perception at time t, and α is a constant denoting the strength of emotional influence. This formulation acknowledges that emotional states can modulate perception (Phelps et al., 2006).

Emotional Memory Systems
The role of emotions in memory encoding and retrieval can be described as:

$$M_{emo}(t) = M(E(t), M(t))$$

In this equation, $M_{emo}(t)$ represents emotional memory at time t, and M is a function combining emotional and other types of memory. This aligns with studies on the emotional modulation of memory (McGaugh, 2004).

Emotional Disorders as Perturbations in Emotional Systems
Emotional disorders can be modeled as disruptions in the emotional system:

$$D(t) = D(E(t))$$

Here, $D(t)$ symbolizes the disorder at time t, and D is a function mapping from emotions to emotional disorders. This conceptualization is consistent with research on affective disorders (Kendler et al., 2003).

References
- Damasio, A. R. (1994). Descartes' error: Emotion, reason, and the human brain. G.P. Putnam's Sons. - LeDoux, J. (1996). The emotional brain: The mysterious underpinnings of emotional life. Simon and Schuster. - Schacter, D. L., Addis, D. R., Buckner, R. L. (2008). Episodic simulation of future events: concepts, data, and applications. Annals of the New York Academy of Sciences, 1124(1), 39-60. - James, W. (1884). What is an emotion? Mind, 9(34), 188-205. - Lange, C. G. (1885). The mechanism of the emotions. The classical psychologists, 672-684. - Damasio, A. (1999). The feeling of what happens: Body and emotion in the making of consciousness. Harcourt Brace. - Cosmides, L., Tooby, J. (2000). Evolutionary psychology and the emotions. Handbook of emotions, 2, 91-115. - Phelps, E. A., Ling, S., Carrasco, M. (2006). Emotion facilitates perception and potentiates the perceptual benefits of attention. Psychological science, 17(4), 292-299. - McGaugh, J. L. (2004). The amygdala modulates the consolidation of memories of emotionally arousing experiences. Annual review of neuroscience, 27, 1-

28. - Kendler, K. S., Gardner, C. O., Prescott, C. A. (2003). Toward a comprehensive developmental model for major depression in men. American Journal of Psychiatry, 160(1), 143-150.

Chapter 5 - Augmenting Symbolic Representations of Neurocognitive Functions with Aspects of Intelligence

Incorporating dimensions of intelligence significantly amplifies the complexity of our mathematical models of the brain. These extended representations facilitate the exploration of how intelligence manifests through neural activities, storage of information, and the simulation of new situations, informed by current understandings in neuroscience and cognitive psychology (Gazzaniga, 2004; Duncan, 2013).

Intelligence as Manipulation of Knowledge
The manipulation of knowledge by neurons can be described as:

$$K'(t) = I_K(K(t), N(t), S(t))$$

In this model, $K'(t)$ represents the new state of knowledge at time t, $K(t)$ is the existing state of knowledge, $N(t)$ is the neuronal state, and $S(t)$ is the simulation state. The function I_K symbolizes how neurons manipulate knowledge to arrive at new understandings. This is consistent with theories that equate intelligence with the ability to adapt and manipulate information (Sternberg, 1985).

Intelligence as Novel Situation Simulation
The capacity to simulate novel situations is captured by:

$$S'(t) = I_S(S(t), N(t))$$

Here, $S'(t)$ represents the new simulation state at time t, and I_S is a function depicting how neurons simulate new scenarios. This aligns with the construct of fluid intelligence, which involves the ability to solve new problems independent of acquired knowledge (Cattell, 1971).

Intelligence as Storage of Information
The storage, distillation, and retrieval of information by intelligence can be described as:

$$I'(t) = I_I(I(t), D(t))$$

In this equation, $I'(t)$ is the new state of stored information at time t, and I_I represents the relevant intelligent processes. This captures the aspect of crystallized intelligence, which involves the accumulation and retrieval of learned knowledge (Horn Cattell, 1966).

Intelligence and Artificial Intelligence
The progress in artificial intelligence (AI) can be modeled as a function over time:

$$AI(t) = \beta \cdot Iprinciples + \gamma \cdot Ineurons$$

16

Here, β and γ are constants, while $I_{principles}$ and $I_{neurons}$ represent our understanding of brain principles and the simulation capabilities of neurons, respectively. This encapsulates the dual nature of progress in AI: conceptual advances and computational fidelity (Russell Norvig, 2016).

Complexity of Intelligence as an Integral Function

The multifaceted nature of intelligence suggests that it is not underpinned by a single mechanism. Therefore, we introduce a composite function to represent the complexity:

$$Intelligence(t) = \int_{mechanisms} I_m(t)\,dm$$

In this formulation, $I_m(t)$ represents different potential mechanisms of intelligence. This model allows for the integration of various aspects, consistent with the notion that intelligence is a complex construct comprising multiple abilities (Gardner, 1983).

References

- Gazzaniga, M. S. (Ed.). (2004). The cognitive neurosciences (3rd ed.). MIT Press. - Duncan, J. (2013). The structure of cognition: Attentional episodes in mind and brain. Neuron, 80(1), 35-50. - Sternberg, R. J. (1985). Beyond IQ: A triarchic theory of human intelligence. Cambridge University Press. - Cattell, R. B. (1971). Abilities: Their structure, growth, and action. Houghton Mifflin. - Horn, J. L., Cattell, R. B. (1966). Refinement and test of the theory of fluid and crystallized general intelligences. Journal of Educational Psychology, 57(5), 253-270. - Russell, S., Norvig, P. (2016). Artificial intelligence: A modern approach. Pearson. - Gardner, H. (1983). Frames of mind: The theory of multiple intelligences. Basic Books.

Chapter 6 - Extending Symbolic Models of Neurocognitive Processes with Time Perception, Sleep, Specialized Systems, and Information Coding

The endeavor to model neurocognitive processes such as intelligence and emotion can be further extended to incorporate various other facets like time perception, sleep, specialized brain systems, consciousness, and neural coding of information. These extensions are informed by empirical evidence and current theories in neuroscience and psychology (Eagleman, 2008; Siegel, 2005; Koch, 2004).

Comparison to Other Species

Intelligence in different species may necessitate distinct mathematical models, accommodating unique aspects such as abstraction and open-ended problem solving in humans. This is consistent with comparative cognition research emphasizing different cognitive architectures across species (Shettleworth, 2010).

Time Representation in the Brain

The perceptual integration of auditory and visual signals for time representation can be modeled as:

$$T(t) = \alpha \cdot A(t) + \beta \cdot V(t)$$

Here, α and β are constants calibrated to account for the typical 30-millisecond difference between auditory and visual processing speeds. This model aligns with studies on multi-sensory integration and time perception (Fujisaki Nishida, 2009).

Sleep and Dreaming

A composite function encapsulating various theories on the function of sleep is:

$$S(t) = \omega \cdot R(t) + \phi \cdot L(t) + \theta \cdot M(t)$$

This model integrates the restorative nature of sleep, memory consolidation, and the possibility of mental simulations (Tononi Cirelli, 2006).

Specialized Systems in the Brain

Given the brain's specialized systems, their combined activity can be represented as:

$$C(t) = \sum_{i=1}^{N} w_i \cdot A_i(t)$$

This is consistent with distributed coding theories that posit that cognition emerges from coordinated activity across specialized networks (Mesulam, 1998). Consciousness

Consciousness can be represented as a function of active and passive neuronal processes:

$$Con(t) = \lambda \cdot Nactive(t) - \mu \cdot Npassive(t)$$

This model lends itself to theories that differentiate between active and passive states in contributing to consciousness (Dehaene Changeux, 2011).

Sleep-Wake Cycle
The sleep-wake cycle can be represented by a sigmoid function:

$$S(t) = \frac{1}{1 + e^{-k(t-\tau)}}$$

This model reflects the biological circadian rhythms governing sleep and wakefulness (Borb´ely Achermann, 1999).

REM Sleep and Memory Consolidation
The state of memory consolidation dependent on REM sleep is modeled as:

$$M(t) = \delta \cdot \int_0^t R(s)ds$$

This is congruent with theories suggesting a role of REM sleep in memory consolidation (Stickgold, 2005).

Coding Information in Spiking Rates
The rate of spiking in neurons can be modeled as a function of external features:

$$R(t) = f(F)$$

This is consistent with rate coding theories in neuroscience (Gerstner et al., 2014).
Neural Networks for Complex Phenomena

Complex phenomena like value judgments can be modeled as:

$$Si = \phi(Xwij \cdot Nj) \sum_{j=1}^{M}$$

This captures the essence of artificial neural networks applied to model complex cognitive phenomena (Rumelhart et al., 1986).

References

- Eagleman, D. M. (2008). Human time perception and its illusions. Current Opinion in Neurobiology, 18(2), 131-136. - Siegel, J. M. (2005). Clues to the functions of mammalian sleep. Nature, 437(7063), 1264-1271. - Koch, C. (2004). The quest for consciousness: a neurobiological approach. Roberts Company. - Shettleworth, S. J. (2010). Cognition, evolution, and behavior. Oxford University Press. -

Fujisaki, W., Nishida, S. (2009). Temporal frequency characteristics of synchrony-asynchrony discrimination of audio-visual signals. Experimental Brain Research, 196(4), 455-464. - Tononi, G., Cirelli, C. (2006).
Sleep function and synaptic homeostasis. Sleep Medicine Reviews, 10(1), 4962. - Mesulam, M. M. (1998). From sensation to cognition. Brain, 121(6), 1013-1052. - Dehaene, S., Changeux, J. P. (2011). Experimental and theoretical approaches to conscious processing. Neuron, 70(2), 200-227. - Borb'ely, A. A., Achermann, P. (1999). Sleep homeostasis and models of sleep regulation. Journal of Biological Rhythms, 14(6), 557-568. - Stickgold, R. (2005). Sleep-dependent memory consolidation. Nature, 437(7063), 1272-1278. - Gerstner, W., Kistler, W. M., Naud, R., Paninski, L. (2014). Neuronal dynamics: From single neurons to networks and models of cognition. Cambridge University Press. - Rumelhart, D. E., Hinton, G. E., Williams, R. J. (1986). Learning representations by back-propagating errors. Nature, 323(6088), 533-536.

Chapter 7 - Advanced Mathematical Models for Memory Storage, Emotional Processing, and Baseline Brain Activity

The endeavor to develop comprehensive mathematical models of brain function must consider several aspects, including memory storage, emotional processing, and the brain's baseline activity. These models are inspired by empirical evidence and theoretical frameworks in neuroscience and psychology (Hebb, 1949; LeDoux, 2000; McClelland et al., 1995).

Neural Population Coding
In population coding, a pattern P is represented across n neurons as $P = (R_1, R_2, ..., R_n)$, where each neuron contributes its spike rate R_i to form the overall pattern. This model is supported by research in neural coding techniques (Georgopoulos et al., 1986).

Cortical Connectivity
Given the extensive connectivity in the cortex, the effective input I to a neuron can be modeled as $I = \sum_{j=1}^{10,000} w_j \cdot S_j$, where w_j are synaptic weights and S_j are signal strengths from connecting neurons. This is consistent with studies on the large-scale connectivity of cortical neurons (Sporns, 2011).

Alternative Signaling Mechanisms
To account for the role of glial cells and biochemical cascades, the total information $T(t)$ can be modeled as $T(t) = \alpha \cdot R(t) + \beta \cdot G(t) + \gamma \cdot B(t)$. These terms are weighted by constants α, β, γ, indicative of the importance of each signaling mechanism (Araque et al., 1999; Purves et al., 2018).

Memory Storage: Synaptic Trace Model
The Synaptic Trace Model posits that memories are formed through synaptic strengthening between co-active neurons. The change in synaptic weight Δw_{ij} can be expressed as $\Delta w_{ij} = \eta \cdot (A_i \cdot A_j)$, embodying Hebbian learning principles ("Cells that fire together, wire together") (Hebb, 1949).

Types and Structures of Memory
Memory types and their associated neural structures can be represented as $M(t, \tau, T) = \sum_{i=1}^{n} \Delta w_{ij} \cdot f(\tau, T)$, where $f(\tau, T)$ denotes how the type and structure of the memory affect its formation (Eichenbaum, 2000).

Memory Associations and Relational Encoding
The relational aspect of memory can be captured by $M_{rel} = {}^P_{i,j} w_{ij} \cdot R(i,j)$, highlighting the role of synaptic weights in encoding relationships between items (Cohen Eichenbaum, 1993).

Memory Retrieval and Destabilization
Memory retrieval can be modeled as $Answer = \rho(Q,M)$, where ρ is a retrieval function scanning memory M based on a query Q. During retrieval, memories may be destabilized, represented by $\Delta M = -\delta \cdot \rho(Q,M)$ (Nader et al., 2000).

Baseline Brain Activity
The brain's baseline activity $B(t)$ can be modeled as $B(t) = \alpha \cdot R(t) + \beta \cdot E(t) + \gamma \cdot F(t)$, incorporating ongoing cognitive functions like restructuring of knowledge $R(t)$, emotional processing $E(t)$, and future simulations $F(t)$ (Raichle et al., 2001).

Task-Specific Deactivation and Resource Allocation
Prior to task engagement, certain brain regions show reduced activity, modeled by $D(t,G) = B(t) - \phi G(t)$. This model underscores the concept of resource allocation (Fox et al., 2005).

Sensory Input as Modifier
Sensory input $S(t)$ may serve as a modifier to baseline activity, represented by $B'(t) = B(t) + \lambda \cdot S(t)$ (Lamme Roelfsema, 2000).

Dreaming and Awake States
Dreaming and awake states can be represented along a continuum as $D(t) = \theta \cdot B(t) + (1-\theta) \cdot S(t)$, balancing the influence of sensory input $S(t)$ on baseline activity $B(t)$ (Hobson, 2009).

Brain as Prognosticator
The brain's ability to simulate futures is captured by $F(t) = \delta \cdot S(t) + (1 - \delta) \cdot M(t)$, emphasizing the role of memories in predictive algorithms (Schacter et al., 2007).

Emotional Processing
Emotional states $E(t)$ can be modeled as $E(t) = \sigma \cdot V(o) + (1-\sigma) \cdot R(s)$, incorporating the value of outcomes $V(o)$ and physiological responses $R(s)$ (Damasio, 1994).

Emotional Disorders
The mathematical representation of emotional disorders, potentially involving neurochemical imbalances or flawed connectivity, remains an active area of research, with implications for understanding conditions like depression and anxiety (Davidson et al., 2002).

These mathematical models serve as foundational structures for understanding complex neurocognitive processes, offering a systematic approach for the scientific community. The aspiration for a "Grand Unified Theory" of brain function remains an ambitious but worthwhile scientific pursuit.

References
- Hebb, D. O. (1949). The Organization of Behavior. John Wiley Sons. LeDoux, J. E. (2000). Emotion circuits in the brain. Annual Review of Neuroscience, 23(1), 155-184. - McClelland, J. L.,

McNaughton, B. L., O'Reilly, R. C. (1995). Why there are complementary learning systems in the hippocampus and neocortex: insights from the successes and failures of connectionist models of learning and memory. Psychological Review, 102(3), 419. - Georgopoulos, A. P., Schwartz, A. B., Kettner, R. E. (1986). Neuronal population coding of movement direction. Science, 233(4771), 1416-1419. - Sporns, O. (2011). The human connectome: a complex network. Annals of the New York Academy of Sciences, 1224(1), 109-125. - Araque, A., Parpura, V., Sanzgiri, R. P., Haydon, P. G. (1999

Chapter 8 - A High-Level Equation for Integrating Multifaceted Brain Functions

The ambition to encapsulate the complexities of brain function into a unified mathematical framework necessitates incorporating many variables. My proposed equation,

$BrainFunction = \alpha{\cdot}NCA + \beta{\cdot}MSR + \gamma{\cdot}BA + \delta{\cdot}FS + \square{\cdot}EMO + \zeta{\cdot}INT + \eta{\cdot}T + \theta{\cdot}SD + \iota{\cdot}SSI + \kappa{\cdot}CON,$

adeptly incorporates various elements that contribute to overall brain function. Here, each term represents a specific aspect, and the coefficients $\alpha,\beta,\gamma,\delta,\square,\zeta,\eta,\theta,\iota,\kappa$ serve as weighting factors. As you suggested, these coefficients could be dynamic, adapting to contextual changes, internal states, or external stimuli.

Neural Coding Activity (*NCA*)
The term *NCA* could encapsulate various aspects of neural coding, such as rate, temporal, and population (Pouget et al., 2000).

$NCA = f(R(t), T(t), P)$

Memory Storage and Retrieval (*MSR*)
MSR would integrate memory storage processes, relational encoding, and retrieval mechanisms (Tulving Craik, 2000).

$MSR = g(\Delta w_{ij}, M_{rel}, \rho(Q, M))$

Baseline Activity (*BA*)
The term *BA* may incorporate the brain's idling activity, which is far from inactive and includes various ongoing cognitive functions (Raichle et al., 2001).

$BA = h(R(t), E(t), F(t))$

Future Simulation (*FS*)
FS would encapsulate the brain's ability to simulate future scenarios, based on sensory input and stored memories (Schacter et al., 2007).

$FS = i(S(t), M(t))$

Emotional State (*EMO*)
EMO could be a composite function of multiple variables reflecting an individual's emotional state, such as physiological responses and emotional memories (LeDoux, 2000).

$EMO = j(V(o), R(s), M_{emo})$

Intelligence (*INT*)
This term would incorporate various dimensions of intelligence, including knowledge manipulation, novel situation simulation, and information storage (Sternberg, 1999).

$$INT = k(K'(t), S'(t), I'(t))$$

Time Representation (*T*)
T would encapsulate how the brain synchronizes auditory and visual signals to create a perception of time (Merchant et al., 2013).

$$T = l(A(t), V(t))$$

Sleep and Dreams (*SD*)
SD would capture various theories and dimensions of sleep, including restorative aspects and memory consolidation (Walker, 2009).

$$SD = m(R(t), L(t), M(t))$$

Specialized Systems Integration (*SSI*)
SSI could represent the coordination of activity levels across various specialized systems within the brain (Sporns, 2011).

$$SSI = n(A_i(t))$$

Consciousness (*CON*)
Finally, *CON* would incorporate active and passive neuronal processes that contribute to conscious experience (Dehaene et al., 2017).

$$CON = o(Nactive, Npassive)$$

This integrative equation aims to offer a comprehensive yet tractable framework for understanding brain function. It holds the promise of harmonizing disparate areas of neuroscience, psychology, and even artificial intelligence, into a coherent theoretical structure. Future empirical studies would be essential to calibrate the weights and validate the functional forms of these terms.

References
- Pouget, A., Dayan, P., Zemel, R. (2000). Information processing with population codes. Nature Reviews Neuroscience, 1(2), 125-132. - Tulving, E., Craik, F. I. M. (Eds.). (2000). The Oxford Handbook of Memory. Oxford University Press. - Raichle, M. E., MacLeod, A. M., Snyder, A. Z., Powers, W. J., Gusnard, D. A., Shulman, G. L. (2001). A default mode of brain function. Proceedings of the National Academy of Sciences, 98(2), 676-682. Schacter, D. L., Addis, D. R., Buckner, R. L. (2007). Remembering the past to imagine the future: the prospective brain. Nature Reviews Neuroscience, 8(9), 657-661. - LeDoux, J. E. (2000). Emotion circuits in the brain. Annual Review of Neuroscience, 23(1), 155-184. - Sternberg, R. J. (1999). Intelligence as developing expertise. Contemporary Educational Psychology, 24(4), 359375. - Merchant, H., Harrington, D. L., Meck, W. H. (2013). Neural basis of the perception and estimation of time. Annual Review of Neuroscience, 36, 313-336. - Walker, M. P.

(2009). The role of sleep in cognition and emotion. Annals of the New York Academy of Sciences, 1156(1), 168-197. - Sporns, O. (2011). The human connectome: a complex network. Annals of the New York Academy of Sciences, 1224(1), 109-125. - Dehaene, S., Lau, H., Kouider, S. (2017). What is consciousness, and could machines have it? Science, 358(6362), 486-492.

Chapter 9 – Summary Exploring the Composite Functions of Brain Activity

Neural Coding Activity (*NCA*) The function $NCA(V,N,C,G)$ encapsulates the complex interplay between voltage spikes V, the number of neurons N, cortical connections C, and the role of glial cells G. These factors collectively contribute to the rate and pattern of neural firing, which encodes information (Liu and Wang, 2001).

Memory Storage and Retrieval (*MSR*) The function $MSR(T,S,E,Q)$ models the role of memory types T, synaptic involvement S, encoding mechanisms E, and retrieval speed Q. Each of these factors plays a critical role in the formation, storage, and retrieval of memories (Eichenbaum, 2017).

Baseline Activity (*BA*) The $BA(O,R,E,D)$ function incorporates the brain's oxygen consumption O, knowledge restructuring R, influence of external stimuli E, and awake dreaming D. These elements collectively contribute to the brain's baseline or 'resting' activity (Raichle, 2015).

Future Simulation (*FS*) The function $FS(P,M,I,A)$ incorporates predictive capabilities P, internal models M, internal expectations I, and the Aristotelian concept of memory A as a tool for future simulation (Schacter and Addis, 2007).

Emotional State (*EMO*) The $EMO(V,U,C,R)$ function encompasses value assignment V, unconscious mechanisms U, cultural influences C, and related disorders R. Each of these variables contributes to the complex landscape of human emotions (LeDoux, 2012).

This framework, although a simplification, offers a structured approach to understanding the multifaceted nature of brain activity. Each function could indeed be a deeply nested equation itself, capturing a myriad of factors and subfactors. Additionally, the equations can be nonlinear, dynamic, and adaptive, subject to temporal and experiential changes.

Applications to Artificial Intelligence
Predictive Modeling Incorporating predictive abilities akin to the brain's future simulation could result in AI systems that are proactive rather than merely reactive. Long Short-Term Memory (LSTM) networks could be further refined to emulate the brain's internal predictive models (Hochreiter and Schmidhuber, 1997).

Neuromorphic Computing Advancements in understanding neural coding could lead to the development of neuromorphic chips that mimic brain-like information processing, potentially surpassing the efficiency of traditional microprocessors for specific tasks (Mead, 1990).
Affective Computing Emulating the emotional landscape of the brain could lead to more empathetic AI systems capable of recognizing and interpreting human emotions (Picard, 1997).

Multi-Modal Learning The brain's adeptness at synchronizing multiple sensory inputs could inform the development of AI systems capable of integrating data from various modalities, enhancing their decision-making capabilities (Baltrusaitis et al., 2019).

Dynamic Memory Allocation Understanding the brain's selective memory encoding could revolutionize AI memory storage, enabling dynamic resource allocation based on task importance (Kanerva, 1988).

Cognitive AI Incorporating facets of human intelligence could lead to AI systems capable of handling complex tasks that require intuition, imagination, or the ability to manage ambiguous data (Marcus, 2018).

Conscious Agents While recreating consciousness in AI remains controversial, insights into its material underpinnings could guide the development of agents with rudimentary self-awareness or introspection (Dehaene et al., 2017).

Real-Time Processing and Integration Emulating the brain's ability to rapidly integrate disparate functions could produce AI systems that excel in real-time data processing, a critical trait for various applications such as autonomous vehicles and financial markets (Mnih et al., 2015).

Sleep and Rejuvenation Algorithms The brain's sleep function, potentially involved in memory consolidation, could inspire algorithms that allow AI systems to optimize their parameters during low-power modes (Hinton et al., 1995).

Context-Aware Processing Mimicking the brain's baseline activity could result in AI systems better equipped for context-aware processing and long-term planning (Bengio et al., 2013).

In summary, the proposed Grand Unified Theory of Brain Function holds significant potential for advancing our understanding of the brain and has myriad applications in the realm of artificial intelligence. Interdisciplinary efforts involving neuroscience, cognitive psychology, computer science, and data science would be essential to realize this promise.

As we reach the end of this monumental journey through the labyrinth of neural pathways and computational equations, one cannot help but appreciate the vastness of human cognition and its immense potential for technological applications. This book has strived to present a comprehensive toolkit for scholars and practitioners in decoding the brain's complexities through mathematical models. However, it is important to acknowledge that the frontiers of neuroscience and AI are continuously expanding. The models and formulas in this book offer a solid foundation, but they are merely the tip of the iceberg. I encourage scholars to build upon this work, fine-tuning and augmenting these mathematical representations to adapt to new discoveries and challenges.

www.ingramcontent.com/pod-product-compliance
Lightning Source LLC
LaVergne TN
LVHW072052060326
832903LV00054B/416